The Gardens Collaborative
c/o Morris Arboretum of the University of Pennsylvania
9414 Meadowbrook Avenue
Philadelphia, PA 19118

ISBN: 0-9653959-0-1

PARADISE
Presented
Beautiful Gardens in Philadelphia and the Delaware Valley

The Featured Gardens of the
Gardens Collaborative:
Thirty of America's Most Spectacular Gardens

Editors
Timothy R. Tomlinson
Barbara Klaczynska, Ph.D.

This book is made possible through the
generous support of The Pew Charitable Trusts.

Introduction

The Featured Gardens
of the Gardens Collaborative:
Thirty of America's Most Spectacular Gardens

N owhere in the United States can you find more beautiful gardens than in Philadelphia, the surrounding Pennsylvania countryside, the small but exquisite state of Delaware, and in the South Jersey communities from the Delaware River to the Pine Barrens. Everywhere you go, from the handsome farmlands in Bucks and Chester Counties, the lavish suburban estates of Montgomery County or the stunning banks of the Brandywine River, colorful flowers, burgeoning woody plants and majestic trees can be found. Early spring casts a lush lime colored blanket on the ground, awaiting May and its harmony of colors – a profusion of azaleas and rhododendrons. Splendid roses appear in June and continue through October; magnificent summer wildflowers flourish; glorious fall foliage foretells the onset of winter with its awesome silhouettes and regal conifers.

What makes this region so horticulturally grand? The rich soil, plentiful rainfall and radiant sunshine are often cited as reasons for the opulent vegetation. Southern plants thrive here because of the warm springs and summers; northern plants receive the sufficient cold needed to succeed.

Perhaps the best explanation is the ardent and skillful gardeners who live and work here. For the past three hundred years, plant enthusiasts have transformed the landscape with

beautiful gardens. Quaker families in Philadelphia, the du Ponts in the Brandywine region and other botanists created green spaces that are now part of our heritage. Garden visionaries and professional designers turned their hand to creating gardens that evolved into modern research and teaching facilities.

Many of the gardens are testimonies to the foresight of their founders and living tributes to the families who lived in them. In many cases, these families endowed the gardens as legacies to public audiences. Chanticleer, developed by the Rosengarten family, incorporates key elements of western garden design. It includes the formal style of French and Italian gardens as well as the naturalistic style. In the same way, Longwood Gardens reflects the dedication of Pierre du Pont who transformed the Peirce family estate into an internationally renowned garden masterpiece. Each year more than one million visitors come to Longwood.

In the same way, other gardens demonstrate the imprint of their founders. Lydia and John Morris created a romantic Victorian landscape that has developed into a paradise-like setting encompassing the Hamilton Fernery, the renowned Rivinus Rose Garden and superb plant and tree collections. Today, as the Morris Arboretum of the University of Pennsylvania, active learning and research is an ongoing part of its operations. Tyler Arboretum evolved from the private horticultural collection of Jacob and Minshall Painter into the oldest and largest arboretum on the East Coast.

The eighteenth century yielded two notable homesteads, Historic Bartram's Garden, the farm of John Bartram, the King's botanist prior to the American Revolution, and Cliveden, a National Trust Property dating from 1763 and the scene of a significant Revolutionary War battle. The Grange Estate and Wyck exemplify houses and gardens that were homes to generations of families who "lived" and loved the properties for centuries. The Rockwood Museum and Ebenezer Maxwell Mansion Victorian Gardens are wonderful Victorian houses that use their gardens as part of energetic interpretative programs that demonstrate how families made these houses their homes. Historic Fallsington, Inc. is a 300-year-old village with over ninety buildings containing many lovely public and private gardens.

The intersection of the garden and other aspects of life is well documented. The healing and rejuvenation qualities of gardening are illustrated in The Lewis W. Barton Arboretum and Nature Preserve at Medford Leas, a beautiful Quaker retirement community, where residents keep active in planning and caring for many lovely courtyards. The Woodlands, on the grounds of the eighteenth century estate of William Hamilton, remains a cemetery and botanic haven, offering a place of peace and solace for the friends and families of the deceased.

The relationship between the arts and nature does not go unnoticed as well. The Barnes Foundation Arboretum was developed to complement, through plant collections and horticultural learning, its world famous collection of art work and art education. The Brandywine Conservancy's Wildflower and Native Plant Gardens provide a beautiful setting for the works of regional artists, the most famous being the Wyeths, exhibited in its museum. Winterthur contains the world's premier collection of American decorative arts in a 983-acre garden that weaves interesting ties between the arts and nature.

A wide variety of educational institutions use arboretums and gardens as their backdrop. The University of Delaware Botanic Gardens and the Henry Schmieder Arboretum of Delaware Valley College are integral parts of excellent educational programs in horticulture and the sciences at their schools. The Quaker tradition of respect for nature is carried out by Haverford College and Scott Arboretum of Swarthmore College. The American College Arboretum surrounds the campus and provides education in insurance and financial services. The Augustinian Fathers have provided education at Villanova University since 1841 and today houses an increasingly expanded Arboretum.

While many of the gardens and arboretums featured in this book have multiple purposes, there are some whose primary mission is to be a public garden. Awbury Arboretum, located in the heart of an urban neighborhood, provides a serene place to walk and reflect.

The Jenkins Arboretum presents a stunning hardwood forest embellished with extraordinary azaleas, rhododendrons and daylilies. Hagley Museum and Library displays a variety of gardens and landscape concepts along the picturesque banks of the Brandywine River, and showcases what was once the world's largest gun powder mill.

The Japanese House and Garden (Shōfusō, The Pine Breeze Villa) with its azaleas, pines, ponds and paths provides a tranquil setting for an outstanding house built to recreate a seventeenth century Momoyama style dwelling. The Taylor Arboretum is located on an old mill site and encompasses a quarry filled with mosses, ferns and wildflowers. In addition to its mansion, The Highlands comprises a lovely garden that draws visitors to what has come to be known as its "secret garden." Interdependent plant communities boasting more than 800 species are maintained in Bowman's Hill Wildflower Preserve. Spectacular seasonal displays showcase native plants unfamiliar to many.

This book is meant as both a keepsake of places you may visit and also as a stimulant to see all thirty gardens, arboreta, historic houses and campuses described in this book. We have not included every garden in the region. We have demonstrated the diversity, beauty and excitement of the many gardens open to public audiences.

Plan to come to these gardens often. Feel free to take a walk by yourself, share a secret with a friend or listen to a child. There are self-guided tours and labeled plants. There are guided programs, workshops, seminars and classes offered at these institutions. Contact the gardens for their hours, admission fees, group tour information and special events. We welcome your visit to the gardens of the Philadelphia - Wilmington region.

7

ACKNOWLEDGEMENTS

The following are photographic credits
for pictures used in this book.

Page 2 - Nick Kelsh
Page 10 - Addison Geary
Page 15 - Laura Keim
Page 19 - Tom Gralish
Page 20 - Frank L. Chance
Page 25 - Judy McKeon
Page 28 - Eric Mitchell
Page 33 - Bob Nichols
Page 46 - The Terry Wild Studio
Page 50 - The Terry Wild Studio
Page 59 - Michael Kah
Page 63 - Larry Albee/Longwood Gardens
Page 64 - D. Fell
Page 66 - Paul Dennison
Page 69 - Linda Eirhart, Courtesy of Winterthur Museum
Page 73 - Herbert Friedman
Page 75 - Property of Historic Fallsington, Inc.
Page 76 - Felice Frankel

Special appreciation to Jeanmarie Foy for her work in the
coordination and proofreading and for her dedication to
the Gardens Collaborative. Thanks to Joanne Dhody
and Mary Madeira of Design Unlimited for their careful
attention to the design and layout of the book.

The Gardens Collaborative is grateful to The Pew Charitable
Trusts, Chanticleer and the Longwood Foundation for their
generosity to our efforts.

Table of Contents

10 Philadelphia and Northwest Suburbs (PA)
12 Awbury Arboretum
14 Cliveden of the National Trust
16 The Highlands Mansion & Gardens
18 Historic Bartram's Garden
20 Japanese House and Garden (Shōfusō, The Pine Breeze Villa)
22 Ebenezer Maxwell Mansion Victorian Gardens
24 Morris Arboretum of the University of Pennsylvania
26 The Woodlands
28 Wyck

30 Main Line (PA)
32 The American College Arboretum
34 The Barnes Foundation Arboretum
36 Chanticleer
38 Haverford College Arboretum
40 The Henry Foundation for Botanical Research
42 Jenkins Arboretum
44 Arboretum Villanova

46 Delaware County (PA)
48 The Grange Estate
50 Scott Arboretum of Swarthmore College
52 Taylor Memorial Arboretum
54 Tyler Arboretum

56 Brandywine Area: Chester County (PA) and Delaware
58 Brandywine Conservancy/Brandywine River Museum
60 Hagley Museum and Library
62 Longwood Gardens
64 Rockwood Museum
66 University of Delaware Botanic Gardens
68 Winterthur Museum, Garden, and Library

70 Bucks County (PA) and New Jersey
72 Bowman's Hill Wildflower Preserve
74 Historic Fallsington, Inc.
76 Medford Leas, The Lewis W. Barton Arboretum and
    Nature Preserve
78 The Henry Schmieder Arboretum of Delaware Valley College

80 Area Map

1. Awbury Arboretum
2. Cliveden of the National Trust
3. The Highlands Mansion & Gardens
4. Historic Bartram's Garden
5. Japanese House and Garden
6. Ebenezer Maxwell Mansion Victorian Gardens
7. Morris Arboretum of the
   University of Pennsylvania
8. The Woodlands
9. Wyck

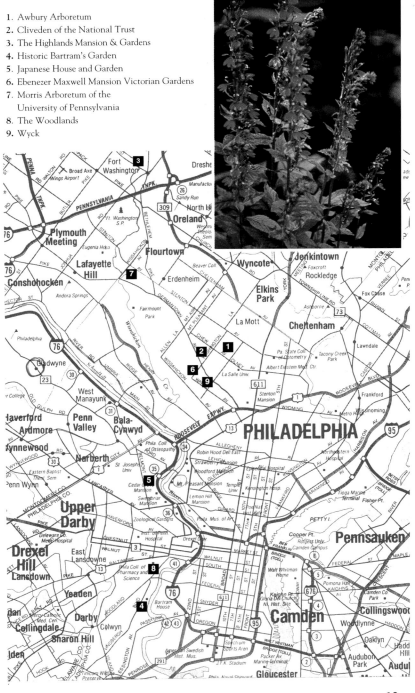

10

P hiladelphia, William Penn's "Greene Country Town," enjoys a 300-year tradition of being a perfect setting for gardens and arboreta. The city is a living history museum with wonderful historic houses including Historic Bartram's Garden and the Japanese House and Gardens located in one of America's largest urban parks, Fairmount Park. The Woodlands offers a rural retreat with its cemetery and mansion that makes the visitor forget bustling West Philadelphia and the University of Pennsylvania campus is across the street.

The northwest part of the city offers historic estates including Cliveden of the National Trust and the Awbury Arboretum and charming small family homes including Wyck and the Ebenezer Maxwell Mansion. The Morris Arboretum of the University of Pennsylvania is a major element in the green space that runs along the Wissahickon Creek. Located a few miles north of the city limits, The Highlands Mansion & Gardens recreates a world of "hunt country" separate from the modern world around it.

AWBURY ARBORETUM

Awbury Arboretum includes an extraordinary fifty-five acres of green space in the historic Germantown section of Philadelphia, and is the largest remaining piece of open land in this part of the city.

Awbury was purchased in 1852 as a summer retreat by Henry Cope, a Quaker businessman and philanthropist, but quickly became a year-round residence for several generations of the Cope family.

The Francis Cope House is the architectural centerpiece of the Arboretum. The picturesque stone cottage with Gothic elements restrained by the Quaker preference for simplicity is one of several houses at Awbury built for family members between 1852 and the 1920s. Today it houses the Arboretum's offices and an exhibit on Awbury's history.

Awbury's grounds were laid out in the 1870s with the help of William Saunders, designer of the cemetery at the Gettysburg Battlefield and of the Capitol grounds in Washington, D.C. In the English landscape garden tradition, clusters of trees were interwoven with open space to make long vistas and visual contrasts.

Today the Arboretum includes open meadows, ponds, woods, and former farmland in addition to the planted landscapes. Hundreds of trees, some of them more than a century old, give visitors a chance to become acquainted with over 140 species.

Much of Awbury was preserved as open space when the Arboretum was established in 1916 as a nonprofit organization. Awbury is now virtually the last nineteenth century estate where a house and its original landscaped grounds remain intact.

Visitors may wish to visit the specimen trees in the Arboretum's English landscape. Haines Field offers a rich diversity of trees to study and enjoy. Awbury's pond is home to a number of wetland species including the State Champion River Birch. Other areas of interest include the Henry Cope Garden and the new Francis Cope House Garden.

Awbury Arboretum
The Francis Cope House
One Awbury Road
Philadelphia, PA 19138-1505
215-849-2855

Hours: Open daily from dawn to dusk. Administrative offices in the Francis Cope House are open Monday through Friday, 9 a.m. until 5 p.m. *Admission:* No charge for admission. For self-guided tours and other information, please stop at the Francis Cope House. Visitors are welcome to walk, jog, and bicycle in the arboretum. Please request permission for large picnics in advance. Guided tours are offered to school groups through Awbury's environmental education programs. Teachers may call 215-849-5561 for details.

CLIVEDEN

Cliveden (1763-67) was constructed for Chief Justice Benjamin Chew as his summer country house in the tradition of the English Palladian villa. The house and grounds were the scene of the Battle of Germantown on October 4, 1777. With a brief exception, Cliveden was continuously occupied by the Chew family until 1972.

The Cliveden property grew from its original eleven acres to more than sixty acres and a working farm during the nineteenth century. Currently the museum occupies the full city block between Johnson and Cliveden Streets along Germantown Avenue – a six-acre haven of lawn, trees, shrubs and flowering borders in the heart of urban northwest Philadelphia.

The grounds complement the grand scale of the eighteenth century house. The graceful landscape is largely twentieth century in origin, marked by tall trees and mature shrubs including sycamore, catalpa, copper beech, holly, magnolia, dogwood, rhododendron and boxwood. Cliveden's *Franklinia* is possibly the largest specimen in the Philadelphia area. Near the Cliveden Street entrance is a formal garden with espaliered fruit trees as well as annuals and perennials. A timeline garden along the carriage house wall highlights plants and gardening styles from the seventeenth to twentieth centuries.

Cliveden's primary architectural feature is the house itself. The grounds were planned to complement and highlight this icon of Philadelphia Georgian architecture. A tree-lined driveway, curving gently from the gate on Germantown Avenue up to the mansion, defines the landscape. The original carriage house and figural garden sculptures survive from the eighteenth century. Remnants of early cold frames, and a twentieth century sundial in the carriage house garden can be found on the property.

Early spring at Cliveden is yellow, with daffodils and forsythia in every direction. Flowering azaleas and small trees also highlight the spring landscape. Dogwoods and rhododendrons enliven Cliveden in the early summer. The perennial garden remains colorful until frost. After the leaves fall, the unshaded house presides prominently over Cliveden's landscape.

Cliveden of the National Trust
6401 Germantown Avenue
Philadelphia, PA 19144
(215) 848-1777   FAX (215) 438-2892

Hours: Grounds are open Monday through Friday from 10 a.m. to 4 p.m., and 12 p.m. to 4 p.m. on weekends. The museum is open for tours Thursdays through Sundays from 12 p.m. to 4 p.m. from April 1-December 31.
Admission: Fee charged. Group rates available. No charge for members of Cliveden or the National Trust for Historic Preservation. No charge for touring the grounds only.

THE HIGHLANDS
MANSION & GARDENS

The Highlands Mansion and Gardens is a forty-four acre estate located twelve miles from downtown Philadelphia. The gardens and landscape are a striking combination of plantings and architecture that have developed over the course of two centuries. Anthony Morris, a Quaker lawyer, built The Highlands in 1796 as a summer house. Since that time four different families have owned the property, each making significant additions to the mansion and gardens. The Highlands' gardens have received praise from a number of sources. A.J. Downing, perhaps the foremost landscape theorist of nineteenth century America, called The Highlands estate, "one of the most remarkable in Pennsylvania," and commented, "This whole estate is a striking example of science, skill, and taste, applied to a country seat, and there are few in the Union superior to it."

In 1917, Caroline Sinkler, an influential woman in Philadelphia society, purchased The Highlands as a country house and installed a two-acre formal garden. The garden included a number of paths, each ending in a focal point of sculpture or statuary. Long herbaceous beds and a central fountain were notable features of her garden, which in 1933 won a Gold Medal for Excellence from the Pennsylvania Horticultural Society.

Today, Caroline Sinkler's garden is dotted with a series of outbuildings and surrounded on three sides by massive stone walls, giving rise to the idea that The Highlands is a secret garden. A unique architectural feature called an exedra, which encloses part of the garden, creates a sort of outdoor room and was reconstructed as part of the Two Hundredth Anniversary celebration of the estate in 1996. The garden also contains an herb parterre.

The Highlands Mansion & Gardens
7001 Sheaff Lane
Ft. Washington, PA 19034
215-641-2687

Hours: The Highlands gardens are open seven days per week from 9 a.m. to dusk, with guided tours available by appointment Monday through Friday, 9 a.m. - 3 p.m.
Admission: Fee charged.

17

HISTORIC BARTRAM'S GARDEN

Tucked away in a hidden corner of urban Philadelphia is an enchanting green oasis rich in botanical history. Only one place on earth can claim the distinction of being America's oldest living botanical garden and that is Historic Bartram's Garden.

American-born Quaker John Bartram (1699-1777), a self-taught expert on the flora of eastern North America, purchased a farm on the Schuylkill River in 1728. When not farming to feed his large family, Bartram traveled the wilds of the American colonies by horseback in search of interesting seeds and plants to bring back to his farm. His goal was to document all the native flora of the New World.

His work earned him the appointment of "Royal Botanist" for North America from King George III. Visitors from around the world flocked to the Garden, including such notables as Benjamin Franklin and George Washington.

Fortunately, Bartram's farm has been preserved virtually unchanged for two centuries, and today it welcomes gardening enthusiasts, history buffs, scholars and schoolchildren. The enchanting forty-four-acre site includes the furnished Bartram house, several unique outbuildings, the botanical garden and a wildflower meadow with a stunning view of the Philadelphia skyline.

A National Historic Landmark, the eighteenth century house features architectural embellishments added by Bartram such as stone columns and carved floral motifs and inscriptions. Outbuildings include the Coach House, Dovecote and the oldest barn in Philadelphia.

The botanical garden features one of the finest collections of native American plants, including the *Franklinia alatamaha* tree, which the Bartrams saved from extinction, and the oldest ginkgo tree in the country.

Visitors can stroll through the Upper Kitchen Garden and fragrant Common Flower Garden and experience a wisteria-draped arbor and the colorful Butterfly and Hummingbird Garden. The grassy hill leading down to the river is dotted with trees such as pawpaw and Carolina silverbells and laced with nature paths. At the river's edge are the remains of a cider press carved from river bedrock.

Historic Bartram's Garden
54th St. and Lindbergh Blvd.
Philadelphia, PA 19143
215-729-5281

Hours: Grounds are open dawn to dusk all year at no charge. House tours and Museum Shop open May-October, Wednesday-Sunday, noon - 4 p.m. and November-April, Wednesday-Friday, noon-4 p.m.
Admission: Fee charged.

THE JAPANESE HOUSE AND GARDEN (SHŌFOSŌ, THE PINE BREEZE VILLA)

Colorful *koi* carp swim in a shallow pond edged by square boulders, and informal steppingstone paths wind between native and imported trees and shrubs. The gentle sound of falling water echoes from the crane island to the miniature hills that frame a "borrowed view" of Memorial Hall and

Fairmount Park. This tranquil setting surrounds the Pine Breeze Villa, a seventeenth-century *shoin* style Japanese house, from which the best views of the garden are achieved. In one corner, an intimate *roji* (tea garden) leads to a ceremonial teahouse, past lanterns and a granite hand-washing basin. From his place by the wall at the northeast end of the garden, a large stone statue of the Buddhist deity Jizo keeps silent watch over the compound. The site of the Japanese House and Garden in West Fairmount Park was first landscaped in Japanese style for the Centennial Exposition of 1876. The current garden, maintained by the Friends of the Japanese House and Garden, was designed by SANO Tansai in 1958 when the House was moved to Philadelphia from the Museum of Modern Art in New York City. For the Bicentennial Celebrations of 1976, the garden was extensively renovated by NAKAJIMA Kenji. The result is one of America's finest and most authentic gardens in the Momoyama style of early seventeenth century Japan.

In summer, cedar, *hinoki* cypress, and pines – white, black, and red varieties – reflect coolly green in the quiet pond. Fall turns the Japanese maples to brilliant crimson, and winter snow coats the stone pagoda and *yukimi* lanterns with pure white. Most visitors, however, seem to enjoy spring, when the blossoms of cherry, plum, dogwood and a brilliant array of white, pink, red, and purple azaleas border the pond.

The Japanese House and Garden (Shōfusō, The Pine Breeze Villa) in The Horticulture Center in West Fairmount Park
North Horticultural Drive at Montgomery Drive
Philadelphia, PA 19131
Mailing address: P.O. Box 2224, Phila., PA 19103
215-878-5097

Hours: Closed November-April. May 1-Labor Day, Tuesday-Sunday, 11 a.m.-4 p.m. September-October, Saturday and Sunday, 11 a.m. - 4 p.m. and by appointment for groups.
Admission: Fee charged. The public is invited to celebrations of each season – Children's Day in early May, the Summer Festival in late June, and tea ceremony demonstrations in October.

EBENEZER MAXWELL MANSION
VICTORIAN GARDENS

The Ebenezer Maxwell Mansion in Historic Germantown is the site of one of the country's first accurately re-created Victorian gardens. The garden provides a sympathetic setting for the eclectic stone villa built by Ebenezer Maxwell in 1859, when Germantown was a rapidly growing suburb, recently opened to development by the commuter rail lines from nearby Philadelphia. Using period plants, the garden was restored in the late 1970s and has now reached glorious maturity with over 150 varieties of trees, shrubs, herbaceous plants, ferns and vines that have been selected according to their availability in Victorian America.

Designed by restoration landscape architect Reed L. Engle, the Mansion's gardens reflect the ideas of the two foremost American garden theorists of the nineteenth century, Andrew Jackson Downing and Frank J. Scott. The Downing Garden represents picturesque garden theories of the 1840s to 1860s. The gently rolling front lawn is planted with irregular groups of rounded shrubs and spire-topped evergreens that screen the house from the street, ensuring privacy while echoing the irregular Gothic forms of the architecture. Two notable features are an iron stag emerging from a thicket of ferns, azaleas and mountain laurel clustered around a small pond and a small yard for drying laundry, enclosed by a clipped privet hedge.

The Scott Garden reflects the more gentle and decorative landscaping taste of the Centennial era. Scott's designs placed ornamental plantings where they would not obscure the views outward from the house. Maxwell's side yard was recontoured to form a broad grass terrace with a "ribbon border" of small shrubs and flowers. An arbor is covered with twining grape vines and a Gothic arch of clipped hemlock forms a gateway into the adjoining yard. Together, the Downing and Scott gardens provide a beautiful period setting for the Victorian mansion.

Ebenezer Maxwell Mansion Victorian Gardens
200 West Tulpehocken Street
Philadelphia, PA 19144
215-438-1861

Hours: The Victorian Gardens at Ebenezer Maxwell
Mansion are accessible to the public at all times. The fully
restored and furnished Mansion is open Friday through
Sunday afternoons, from March to December, and at all
other times to groups, by appointment.
Admission: Fee charged to tour the house.
Entrance to the gardens is free.

23

MORRIS ARBORETUM
OF THE UNIVERSITY OF PENNSYLVANIA

Within its ninety-two public acres, thousands of rare and lovely woody plants, including many of Philadelphia's oldest and largest trees, are set in a romantic Victorian landscape garden of winding paths, streams, and special garden areas. Visitors discover hidden grottos, fountains, and Japanese rockwork, stroll through a formal rose garden or the elegant glasshouse fernery, explore native woodland areas or collect ideas for trees that will thrive in urban areas. A group of schoolchildren is glimpsed through the window of a diminutive log cabin; they are learning about how early Americans used plants as medicine. In the cottage garden, an Arboretum class is in full swing, learning the basics of perennial gardening.

The Morris Arboretum of the University of Pennsylvania began in 1887 as "Compton," the summer home of John and Lydia Morris, brother and sister. The land the Morrises purchased in Chestnut Hill was barren, with poor soil that drained too quickly; but with diligent care they surrounded their home with a landscape and plant collection devoted to beauty and knowledge. It was their dream that their estate one day be a place of study, with a school and laboratories devoted to horticulture and botany.

Exploring the new world of knowledge available to Victorians, John and Lydia traveled widely, bringing ideas, artwork, crafts and plants back to Compton. The Morrises established a tradition of placing sculpture in the garden that continues today. Compton became the Morris Arboretum of the University of Pennsylvania in 1932. Today, Morris Arboretum is an interdisciplinary resource center for the University and is recognized as the official arboretum of the Commonwealth of Pennsylvania. Science, art, and humanities are pursued through a variety of research, teaching, and outreach programs that link the Arboretum to a world-wide effort to nurture the earth's forests, fields and landscapes.

Morris Arboretum
of the University of Pennsylvania
100 Northwestern Avenue
Philadelphia, PA 19118
215-247-5777

Hours: "A garden for all seasons," the Arboretum
welcomes visitors year-round, except for the week between
Christmas and New Year's. Hours: 10 a.m. - 4 p.m. daily,
Monday through Sunday. Open until 5 p.m. on
Saturdays and Sundays, April-October.
Admission: Fee charged. Free to members and students,
faculty and staff of the University of Pennsylvania.
Free admission to all on Saturday mornings until noon.
Special guided tours for the public are held on
Saturdays and Sundays year-round at 2 p.m.;
other tours are available by reservation.

THE WOODLANDS

Since its transformation into a "rural" cemetery in 1840, the garden landscape of The Woodlands has offered the living the unique experience of beauty, peace and recollection as a "space apart" from the clamor of the moment. It is a green urban oasis which serves as a "landscape of memory" for visitors strolling its fifty-five designed acres of Victorian garden cemetery along grass-covered brick walkways and curving drives. Here, refreshed by its greenery, they may read the history of Philadelphia and the nation in the stone reminders of those resting in the pleasures of the garden eternal.

In the spring, the greenery of The Woodlands is punctuated by the bright hues of azaleas, dogwoods, flowering cherries and rhododendrons; summer brings hikers, joggers, mothers and babies in perambulators, bikers, skaters and strolling families from the nearby universities and neighborhoods enjoying the perennial beds planted and maintained by local garden groups; fall offers the changing colors of ginkgoes, oaks, tulip poplars and other special plantings along with picnickers, Halloween revelers, photographers, and outdoor dance performances until the white blanket of winter leaves only a forest of towering marble obelisks and the occasional holiday decoration to mark the landscape until the return of spring.

At the Woodlands, before the cemetery, William Hamilton (1745-1813) created one of the most spectacular picturesque English-style landscape gardens in America with an unsurpassed collection of non-native "exotics," including first imports of the ginkgo, ailanthus, Lombardy poplar and Norway maple. Praised by visitor and botanical correspondent Thomas Jefferson as "the chastest model of gardening which I have ever seen out of England," memories of that earlier landscape exist in the design of the grounds, scattered offspring of those first plantings and above all, in a visit to Hamilton's spectacular eighteenth century Adamesque mansion. The mansion's floor plan establishes a special visual dialogue with the surrounding landscape through its great windows and reflecting mirrors.

A National Historic Landmark, the house and its matching eighteenth century carriage house/stable are, along with the landscape, The Woodlands Heritage National Historic Trail and will soon be part of a Schuylkill River Botanic Trail joining other historically-significant botanical sites on the river's western shore along a greenway/bike path.

The Woodlands
4000 Woodland Avenue
Philadelphia, PA 19104
215-386-2181

Hours: Grounds are open every day 9 a.m.- 5 p.m., mansion 9 a.m.-5 p.m. weekdays or by appointment.
Admission: No charge for admission. Fee charged for guided tours. Ample parking is available on the grounds. Easily accessed by public transportation.

WYCK

Wyck, a National Historic Landmark, was the home to nine generations of the same Quaker Philadelphia family, the Wistars and Haineses from 1690-1973. Its grounds include a nationally known garden of old roses which grow in their original plan dating from the 1820s.

Wyck's colonial house, remodeled in 1824 by the architect William Strickland, and its gardens give an over-view of the history of the way of life in this family, and of Philadelphia

history, using the furnishings and possessions accumulated over 300 years as illustrations. Significant eighteenth and nineteenth century furniture, ceramics, and needlework bring alive the comforts and tastes of the time. Botanical and natural history collections and the family's extensive library of early horticultural and agricultural volumes are also noteworthy. Although Wyck is now located in an urban area, visitors are given a sense of the earlier rural landscape with a woodlot, vegetable and herb gardens, and ornamental gardens as well as original outbuildings which include a smokehouse, icehouse and coach house. The house itself was designed to "bring the outside in," each room being only one room deep allowing maximum light and air. The central conservatory with its large, sliding glass pocket doors overlooks the lawn and a park-like setting of trees on one side and the rose garden on the other.

The family's special interest and involvement in horticulture and natural history is apparent in their collections and library. Many of the family pursued careers in horticulture and natural history – Reuben Haines III was a founder of the Pennsylvania Horticultural Society and the Academy of Natural Sciences; his granddaughter, Jane Bowne Haines founded the School of Horticulture for Women. The history of these individuals, the landscape and gardens are well documented in the Wyck Papers and through photographs of the garden over time. This is one of the only gardens in the country which has not been altered since the 1820s. The garden is at its peak in late May and early June when the roses are in bloom.

WYCK
6026 Germantown Avenue
Philadelphia, PA 19144
215-848-1690

Hours: April 1st-December 15th, Tuesday, Thursday, Saturday, 1- 4 p.m. and year-round by appointment.
Admission: Fee charged.

10. The American College Arboretum
11. The Barnes Foundation Arboretum
12. Chanticleer
13. Haverford College Arboretum
14. The Henry Foundation for
    Botanical Research
15. Jenkins Arboretum
16. Arboretum Villanova

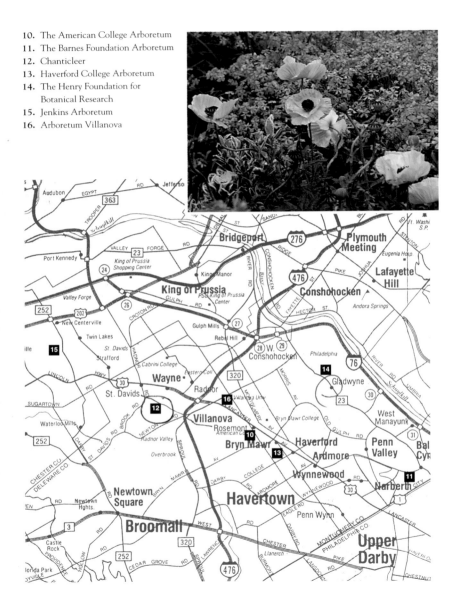

T his world-famous suburban area is replete with a range of communities which includes active towns, modest villages, magnificent schools, colleges and universities, and grand estates.

Named for the tracks of the Pennsylvania railroad around which its commuter suburbs developed, the Main Line offers a stately setting for the many college arboreta and estate gardens scattered throughout its area. Chanticleer, the Jenkins Arboretum and The Henry Foundation for Botanical Research offer gardens lovingly created by families and opened to public audiences. The beautiful arboreta of The American College, Barnes Foundation, Haverford College and Villanova University provide settings for their educational endeavors.

THE AMERICAN COLLEGE ARBORETUM

Developed as an arboretum, The American College's thirty-five-acre campus is noted for a collection of over 600 labeled specimen trees that form the backdrop for a wooded stream valley, a pond and developing gardens. Once the site of several large estates, the property is graced with fine old trees. Over the years, additional trees planted by graduating classes and in honor of individuals have added to the arboretum's diversity of species.

When the College purchased the property in 1959, the Trustees recognized that the existing landscape provided opportunities for developing a horticultural treasure. From the beginning, stewardship of this landscape was a priority. Renowned architects, Aldo Giurgola and Ehrman Mitchell, prepared a master plan for the site and designed the primary buildings, resulting in a visually cohesive campus. Their sensitive design preserved the site's original character. Placement of the College buildings horizontally along the crests of the hills encloses the stream valley and expansive lawns, creating a sense of internal space and allowing nature to flow through the center of the campus. The architecture has received national and international recognition.

Education is as important here as visual enjoyment. Each tree in the arboretum has an accession tag indicating its botanical and common name; 150 selected trees are high-lighted with larger labels that include the common name, botanical name, plant family, and native habitat of the tree.

A seasonal feature of the arboretum includes extensive plantings of unusual annuals, perennials, and vegetables – all carefully labeled – which are cultivated in a cottage garden, and in special flower beds, borders, and containers.

Open year-round, the arboretum is a place of beauty in every season. Visitors are encouraged. Paved paths provide easy access. Benches offer a place to rest amid towering trees, expanses of lawn, and serene views.

The American College Arboretum
270 South Bryn Mawr Avenue
Bryn Mawr, PA 19010
610-526-1228 610-526-1100 (Information on weekends)

Hours: The arboretum is open from dawn to dusk every day.
Group tours are available by appointment.
Admission: No charge for admission.

THE BARNES FOUNDATION

The Barnes Foundation was established by Dr. Albert C. Barnes in 1922 as an educational institution, to "promote the advancement of education and appreciation of the fine arts." The art gallery contains more than 2,500 art objects, including more than 800 paintings. Selected for their aesthetic value, the collections of flowering plants were created to supplement the Foundation's art appreciation classes and the Arboretum's School. John Dewey, the first Director of Education at the Foundation, described the goal of the institution: "the art gallery *and* the arboretum make a *unit* each of definite educational value, and one must reinforce the other if the Foundation is to attain the ideal of making a place that would serve as a model for institutions and cities which desire to make art and trees and flowers positively educational as well as aesthetic."

The Barnes Foundation Arboretum is noted for its diversity of species and varieties, including many rare and mature specimens, growing on a modest twelve-acre property. The previous owner, Captain Joseph Lapsley Wilson, had established an arboretum on the property between 1880 and 1922, and many of Captain Wilson's specimen trees remain today. These include cedar of Lebanon, katsura tree, European beech cultivars, Japanese raisin tree, and ginkgo tree. Genera well represented by large numbers of species include maple, buckeye or horse chestnut, dogwood, holly, magnolia, oak and viburnum. There are many genera of conifers of which fir, spruce and pine are well represented. The arboretum includes a woodland, plantings of crabapples and stewartias, a rose garden, peony garden and more than 250 varieties of lilacs.

Flower gardens established in the 1930s and 1940s have been restored to their original plans using as much authentic plant material as possible to create the same color and spatial relationships as the original gardens. These gardens include an annual garden, formal gardens with rock garden plants growing in rock walls, and a rose garden. Most of the herbaceous plant material is grown from seed in the Arboretum's greenhouse.

The Barnes Foundation Arboretum
300 North Latch's Lane
Merion, PA 19066
610-667-0290

Hours: Open on Thursday, 12:30-5 p.m.; Friday, Saturday, Sunday, 9:30 a.m. - 5 p.m.
Admission: Fee charged. Please note: Hours and admission fees are subject to change. Please call to confirm.

CHANTICLEER

The history of Chanticleer begins with Adolph Rosengarten, Sr., head of a chemical company that later merged with Sharp and Dohme to become part of the Merck pharmaceuticals empire. In 1912, Mr. Rosengarten bought seven acres of land in St. Davids near Philadelphia and moved his family to the estate in 1913. Over the years, the acreage was expanded and consolidated into a thirty-acre estate by Adolph Rosengarten, Jr., and his wife, Janet.

Adolph Rosengarten, Jr. died in 1990. He left his property to be developed and managed by the Chanticleer Foundation. Now a "pleasure garden," Chanticleer has undergone an almost total transformation.

Thousands of bulbs clothe the ground in spring, orchards of flowering trees follow, with native wildflowers blooming in the woods. A vegetable garden complements a cut-flower garden, both accompanied by espaliered fruit trees. Court-yards are a framework for unusual combinations of herba-ceous perennials, punctuated by pots of tropical plants. Roses grow in formal beds dressed with bulbs and annual and perennial plants. Vines grow in nooks and crannies, trailing and twining. Sun-loving wildflowers decorate a meadow while a perennial garden reaches its peak in the warmest days of summer. A woodland garden carpeted with exotic groundcovers and full of rarities precedes a water garden surrounded by grasses and sweet-smelling herbs. Unusual benches invite the visitor to relax in the shade of plant draped arbors. A sharp frost closes the garden. Come again in spring.

Chanticleer
786 Church Road
Wayne, PA 19087
610-687-4163

Hours: April through October, Wednesday-Saturday, 10 a.m. -3:30 p.m. You do not need an appointment to visit the garden; guided tours for ten or more people, Wednesday-Thursday, 10 a.m. & 1:30 p.m., by reservation only.
Admission: A contribution is suggested.

HAVERFORD COLLEGE ARBORETUM

In the late seventeenth century, Welsh Quakers settled upon 40,000 acres of land, ceded to them by William Penn, and planned to establish a barony. Eventually their endeavor failed, and the Welsh Tract, so-called, was divided. In 1831, a distinguished group of Philadelphia and New York Quakers purchased a tract of land with significant natural beauty. Upon this gently rolling farmland, which included open spaces, woodlands and streams, Haverford College was founded.

William Carvill, an English gardener, was hired in 1834 to convert the farmland into a functioning college campus, and he did so with great style and beauty. His design, still evident today, reflected the influence of Sir Humphry Repton, one of England's great landscape architects. William Carvill planted a diverse collection of trees to frame and accent the sweeping vistas. The all-volunteer Campus Club further developed Carvill's plan from 1901 to the late 1960s. The Campus Arboretum Association, founded in 1974, continues the mission of campus preservation and beautification.

On 216 acres, Haverford features majestic trees, historic buildings, nature trails and a duck pond which attracts interesting wildlife. Over 1,000 trees and shrubs are adorned with identification labels containing information on nomenclature and native habitat. The Pinetum offers a selection of conifers of particular interest to botanists and horticulturists. Benches dot the campus in places conducive to appreciating the landscape design or inspiring thought, and they provide a tranquil respite for botanical wayfarers.

Of special interest are three Pennsylvania State Champion Trees and a traditional Japanese Zen garden which offers quiet contemplation. Along the nature trail, the Ryan Pinetum hosts 330 conifers for lush year-round growth and botanical interest. The Herb Garden is a special highlight.

Inspired by the English parks of the nineteenth century, the Arboretum incorporates a design of interest during all seasons of the year.

Haverford College Arboretum
Haverford College
370 Lancaster Avenue
Haverford, PA 19041
610-896-1101

Hours: Open dawn to dusk 365 days a year.
Admission: No charge for admission. The Campus
Arboretum Association offers self-guided nature walks,
guided tours, garden visits, educational
classes and lectures.

THE HENRY FOUNDATION
FOR BOTANICAL RESEARCH

If any garden site can be said to be a study in contrasts, The Henry Foundation uniquely fits that description. Its fifty acres of spectacular views and dazzling plantings are just a few miles from Center City Philadelphia but situated in splendid isolation.

The grounds are rugged, with rough terrain enlivened by steep slopes and giant boulders with massive outcroppings crowning the highest point, site of the gem-like rock garden. Yet from the terrace of the Foundation's stone and gabled headquarters are sweeping views of meadows, trees and sky.

The diversity of the terrain creates amazing microclimates for plants from such widely disparate locations as northern British Columbia, the "Tropical Valley" at 69-degrees north, to items from Texas, Florida and Nova Scotia.

Among the most popular and noteworthy native plants are magnolia, snowbell, rhododendron, silverbell, sweet shrub, white fringetree and yellowwood. Other specialties of interest are phlox, trillium and native wildflowers. During winter the colorful gathering of the blooming amaryllidaceae species, primarily from South America and continuing to Chile, is a surprising delight.

The Henry Foundation was founded in 1948 by Mary Gibson Henry, a highly respected field botanist and plantswoman. For more than forty years she traveled the North American continent with a keen eye and sharp digging tools selecting superior forms of known and unknown plants. The result of her pioneering efforts is an unparalleled collection of native plants.

The Foundation has welcomed visitors from throughout the world including scholars from China, botanists, academics, naturalists, artists, nature photographers, and tour groups. But by far, the majority of the Foundation's visitors are couples and individuals who find a surprising oasis of spectacular beauty in a garden that began as the delight of a single family, became a preserve of professional naturalists, and now is available to everyone.

With undiminished zeal, the Foundation tradition continues, searching the field for distinctive plants to complement the unique array of flora in these naturalistic settings. Many of the plants are now being propagated for distribution to botanical gardens and responsible growers here and abroad.

The Henry Foundation for
Botanical Research
801 Stony Lane
P.O. Box 7
Gladwyne, PA 19035
610-525-2037

Hours: The arboretum is open Monday through Friday, 10:00 a.m. to 4:00 p.m. Other times for group tours by appointment.
Admission: No charge for admission or parking.

JENKINS ARBORETUM

The Jenkins Arboretum is not a converted estate garden but rather an existing remnant of the once continuous Southeastern Pennsylvania hardwood forest. The mixed

hardwood forest ecosystem, including a large pond and stream, was carefully developed as a public garden and opened in 1976. Large natural stands of mountain laurel, pinxterbloom azalea, blueberry, deerberry, and other heath family plants flourished at this site. Vast quantities of beautiful azaleas and rhododendrons were planted when Jenkins became a public garden while still preserving a large diversity of the existing native flora.

Native flora from Eastern North America is prominently featured as the overall ornamental style of landscape design. The purpose of the Arboretum was not to try to recreate an ecological perspective on Penn's Woods but rather to display broad botanical diversity within an existing ecology. Although many plantings are naturalized, the Jenkins Arboretum has a definite garden appearance.

The Jenkins Arboretum displays its chosen specialization of the genus Rhododendron with more than 150 different species from all over the world. This includes evergreen and deciduous azaleas as well as small and large-leafed rhododendrons. Large drifts of all the Eastern North American deciduous azalea species provide wonderful color in both the spring and the fall. All totalled, there are over 4000 azaleas and rhododendrons with something in bloom from March until October with the month of May the peak season.

A tremendous springtime display of thousands of azaleas and rhododendrons as well as ferns and wildflowers awaits visitors. Paved walkways allow comfortable public access yet still preserve the delicate forest ecology. The walkways are ideal for strollers and visitors of all ages. There is always something of interest throughout the year.

Jenkins Arboretum
Elisabeth Phillippe Jenkins Foundation
631 Berwyn Baptist Road
Devon, PA 19333
610-647-8870

Hours: The Arboretum is open from sunrise to sunset, every day of the year.
Admission: No charge for admission. However, donations are greatly appreciated.

ARBORETUM VILLANOVA

The arboretum at Villanova University was dedicated in 1993, however, the beauty of the landscape has been in place, in some cases, for over 100 years. The campus covers 222 acres on the Main Line and offers diverse settings for many different species of trees. The collection consists of over 1,500 trees representing approximately 100 species growing on University grounds, complemented by many flowering annuals and perennials.

Springtime is a special seasonal cycle at Villanova. From almost any point on campus, one can view at least one daffodil. Over 35,000 bulbs have been planted and are bright spots of sunshine even on the gloomiest days. Flowering pear, crabapple, cherry and horse chestnut trees herald the vernal transition. Arboretum Villanova recalls and preserves the historic beauty of the campus, provides for continued beautification to enhance the academic environment and establishes the arboretum as a source of pride within the community, and educates about the diversity, environmental benefits and aesthetic qualities of plant materials.

All seasons offer their special qualities in the arboretum. The trademark tree, the beech, is equally impressive whether in full leaf or in dormancy. Their structures, in any season, are quite impressive. A cut-leaf Japanese maple has been sculptured over the years and is a very large specimen. Dawn redwoods flourish on the grounds as well as a Giant redwood.

Ryan's Way, a memorial to a unique arboretum guardian and alumnus, redefines the main entrance to the campus and is marked by stone sitting walls, willow oaks, native shrubs and perennial flowers. The guiding philosophy of the arboretum is to strive to plan for the future with respect to our past.

Arboretum Villanova
Villanova University
800 Lancaster Avenue
Villanova, PA 19085
610-519-4426

Hours: The Arboretum is open every day from dawn to dusk.
Admission: No charge for admission.

17. The Grange Estate
18. Scott Arboretum of
    Swarthmore College
19. Taylor Memorial Arboretum
20. Tyler Arboretum

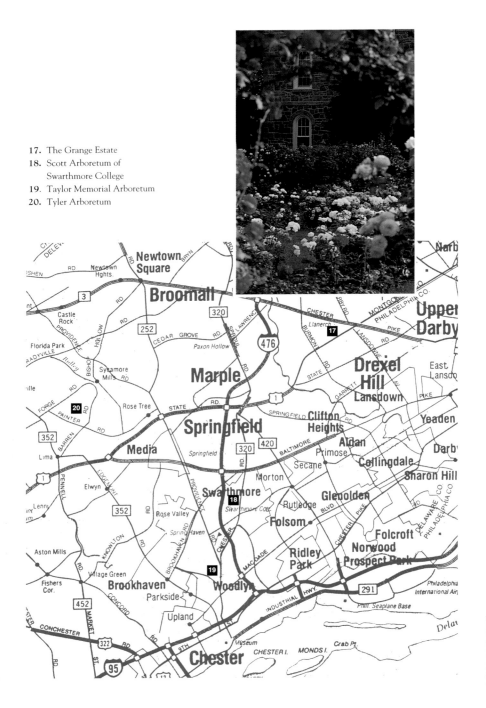

Dispersed throughout this county's busy residential and commercial areas can be found magnificent estates, preserves and institutions that create worlds of quiet and beauty. Swarthmore College boasts one of the most beautiful campuses on the East Coast enhanced by its Scott Arboretum. Tyler Arboretum and Taylor Arboretum are situated on the banks of the Ridley Creek while The Grange Estate dominates its setting on the Cobbs Creek.

THE GRANGE ESTATE

Nestled in the hillside overlooking Cobb's Creek, The Grange is one of the many notable country seats surrounding Philadelphia. The Grange was first settled in 1682 by Henry Lewis, a Welsh Quaker, one of the first three European settlers in Haverford Township. The first section of the present mansion was built about 1710. The garden legacy of The Grange dates to the 1750s when Charles Cruickshank began the landscape design, carving the terraced gardens from the hillside. The gardens are protected from above by the high stone rear wall of the eighteenth century Long Barn and are bordered below by the cucumber magnolia, Japanese pagoda, and ginkgo trees, now of record size in Pennsylvania. In the 1780s John Ross, prominent financier of the American Revolution expanded the gardens and entertained many influential men of the time at his country seat.

Today, The Grange Estate enchants visitors, allowing them to step back to the time of former owners for whom The Grange was a retreat from the hurried pace of city life. The Grange mansion rises majestically in nineteenth century Gothic splendor from the hillside, bounded to the south by the eighteenth century gardens and to the north by the woodland stand of stately tulip poplar, oak and beech. The Grange's outbuildings are nestled into the landscape, each with a story of its own to tell. The gardens and grounds are as beautiful as they were in centuries past, first with the early snowdrops and winter aconites, followed by the spring bulbs, flowering trees and wildflowers, then the peonies in late May and roses in early June. The annuals, complemented by the soft hues of the perennials provide a burst of color through the summer months into early fall. The variety of tree species provides a backdrop of many shades of green until Nature in autumn touches the leaves with her brush of reds and golds.

The Grange Estate is owned by the Township of Haverford and is listed on the National Register of Historic Places. It is one of the treasured public sites in Delaware County.

The Grange Estate
Myrtle Avenue and Warwick Road
Havertown, PA 19083
610-446-4958

Hours: Open weekends April-October. Tours are approximately one hour. The last tour leaves the Mansion at 3 p.m.

Admission: Fee charged. For arrangement for special tours including school and theme tours, rentals and off-site presentations call The Grange Hotline at 610-446-4958.

49

SCOTT ARBORETUM OF SWARTHMORE COLLEGE

The Scott Arboretum is a garden of suggestions, covering more than 300 acres of the Swarthmore College campus. The Arboretum grows over 3,000 different kinds of plants, which create the College landscape and provide a display of the best trees, shrubs and perennials recommended for gardens in the Delaware Valley.

Established in 1929 as a living memorial to Arthur Hoyt Scott, Class of 1895, the Scott Arboretum is open to the public year-round so gardeners may visit during every season to view the many plant highlights. There is always something of interest at the Arboretum—the first crocus of spring, the roses in summer, or the snow covered hollies in winter. Swarthmore College is the first school to develop its campus as an arboretum to educate by visual demonstration the beauty of plants that can be cultivated by the average home gardener.

To make comparisons of plant varieties easier, groups of plants are grown together in collections. To supplement this, plants are labeled with both their common and scientific names. Major plant collections include: flowering cherries, conifers, corylopsis, crabapples, daffodils, dogwoods, hydrangeas, hollies, lilacs, maples, magnolias, native azaleas, oaks, quinces, rhododendrons, roses, tree peonies, vibur-nums, wisterias and witch-hazels.

Other areas of special note are the Terry Shane Teaching Garden, the Scott Entrance Garden, the Dean Bond Rose Garden, the Sue Schmidt Garden, the Theresa Lang Garden of Fragrance, the Harry Wood Courtyard Garden, the Winter Garden, and the Cosby Courtyard. An outstanding landscape feature at the Arboretum is the Scott Outdoor Amphitheater where commencement is held each spring and free summer concerts are staged.

Seasonal highlights include winter: hollies, Winter Garden, amphitheater, pinetum; spring: bulbs, cherries, magnolias, lilacs, azaleas, crabapples, tree peonies and viburnums; summer: Summer Bloom Border, Entrance Garden, Teaching Garden, Rose Garden, Fragrance Garden, hydrangeas; fall: majestic trees with fall color, crabapples, Crum Woods, viburnums.

Scott Arboretum of Swarthmore College
Swarthmore College
500 College Avenue
Swarthmore, PA 19081-1397
610-328-8025

Hours: The Arboretum grounds are open year-round, dawn to dusk. Office hours are Monday-Friday, 8:30 a.m. - noon, 1-4:30 p.m Closed Friday afternoons June-August, July 4, Thanksgiving (Thursday & Friday), week of December 25-January 1.
Admission: No charge for admission.

TAYLOR MEMORIAL ARBORETUM

Taylor Memorial Arboretum – a thirty-acre preserve located along Ridley Creek in historic Delaware County, Pennsylvania – was established in 1931 by Joshua C. Taylor, a prominent Chester lawyer and banker, to promote the "health, enjoyment and education of the public in perpetuity."

The property has been managed since 1986 by Natural Lands Trust, a nonprofit regional land trust dedicated to working with people to conserve land in the Philadelphia metropolitan region and other nearby areas of environmental concern. The Arboretum features several interesting natural elements, provides habitat for a variety of wildlife, and contains an extensive collection of unusual plants.

Anne's Grotto, a former quarry site, shelters ferns, wildflowers and azaleas. A waterfall and millrace – built on the property in 1740 by Daniel Sharpless to power his sawmill, grist mill, fulling mill and dyeworks – now feed the Bald Cypress Pond, which is filled with cattails, rushes and irises. The pond also provides habitat for frogs, snakes, turtles and a variety of waterfowl. The preserve's woodlands, which are brimming with tulip, oak, ash, beech, cherry and hickory trees, include an understory of holly, viburnum and spicebush. Meadows of red top grasses, little bluestem, goldenrod and blue vervain provide additional habitat for wildlife.

Visitors will enjoy the turf and mulch trails that wind through plant collections featuring azaleas, dogwoods, magnolias, junipers, lilacs, viburnums, witchhazels, Japanese maples, boxwoods and arborvitae. Three Pennsylvania State Champion trees – needle juniper, giant dogwood and lacebark elm – are located on the property and sure to delight arbor enthusiasts.

Taylor Memorial Arboretum
10 Ridley Drive
Wallingford, PA 19086
610-876-2649

Hours: Open daily 9 a.m. - 4 p.m. except major holidays.
Admission: No charge for admission.

TYLER ARBORETUM

Visitors who regularly return to Tyler Arboretum often mention the arboretum's atmosphere of spiritual repose as the quality that draws them back. An aura of tranquility reigns over the 650-acre property near Media, Pennsylvania, that can be explained in part by the arboretum's Quaker beginnings. Dating back to a 1681 land grant, the property remained in the same family for over 250 years. A manor house built in 1738 holds the furnishings owned by eight generations, although renovations made to "Lachford Hall" over the years attest to everchanging notions of style.

The unique stamp of the arboretum's character, however, owes itself to the Painter brothers, Minshall and Jacob, who owned and farmed the property in the mid-1800s. Industrious and intellectually curious, the two Quaker brothers pursued their hobby of horticulture with gusto, planting the valley behind their house with more than a thousand shrubs. About twenty of the Painters' original trees still stand, including a cedar-of-Lebanon whose arching branches gracefully frame vistas of the original home-stead, and the towering giant sequoia which serves as the arboretum's living symbol.

While breathtaking displays of rhododendrons, magnolias, maples, cherries, crabapples and lilacs greet visitors through-out the seasons – especially in spring – much of the property remains a secret to be slowly discovered and enjoyed at

leisure. Extensive trails with names such as Dismal Run, Rocky Run, Dogwood and Pink Hill invite exploration. Great stands of oak, tulip poplar and beech march up and down hillsides, and shelter unexpected ruins from the past. A brook babbles over a rocky valley bed. Needled conifers dot vast and solemn stretches of meadow grasses. Pink mountain phlox decorate one of the last of the area's serpentine barrens.

Yet if time seems to stand still throughout much of the arboretum, Tyler is home to an ongoing panoply of life. The croaks and calls of wildlife pierce the Quaker quiet. Groups of giggling school children gather around the trunks of giant trees. The carefully tended Fragrant, Bird and Butterfly Gardens reflect continuum and reverence for life.

Tyler Arboretum
515 Painter Road
Media, PA 19063-4424
610-566-5431

Hours: Arboretum grounds open daily 8 a.m.-dusk (varies seasonally from 5-8 p.m.).
Admission: Fee charged. Members are admitted free.

21. Brandywine Conservancy /
    Brandywine River Museum
22. Hagley Museum and Library
23. Longwood Gardens
24. Rockwood Museum
25. University of Delaware
    Botanic Gardens
26. Winterthur Museum,
    Garden and Library

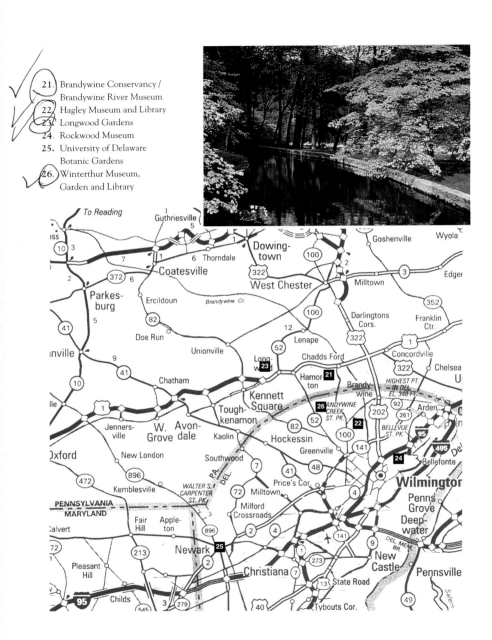

T he Brandywine Area encompasses the southeastern tip of Pennsylvania and the state of Delaware and offers a setting that draws millions of visitors each year for its natural beauty, historical past and wonderful gardens. Hagley Museum and Library and Winterthur offer combinations of historic buildings and gardens set against spectacular natural backgrounds designed to complement each other in display settings. Longwood Gardens is a beacon offering one of the largest conservatories in the world as well as outdoor landscapes that encompass carefully manicured backdrops and miles of naturalistic trails. Rockwood Museum outside of Wilmington offers lovely garden settings and the University of Delaware Botanic Gardens offers interesting gardens for educational and aesthetic purposes.

BRANDYWINE CONSERVANCY/
BRANDYWINE RIVER MUSEUM

The Brandywine Conservancy's Wildflower and Native Plant Gardens at the Brandywine River Museum are a living representation of the Conservancy's mission to preserve, protect, and share American artistic, natural, and historical resources, principally those of the Brandywine region.

The gardens are an extensive collection of wildflowers and native plants that are displayed in a naturalistic style. Surrounding the Conservancy's Brandywine River Museum and parking areas, the use of native plants in public spaces is demonstrated. In addition, around the buildings of the Environmental Management Center and the Membership and Garden Offices, visitors may view native plants displayed on a scale similar to the home landscape.

The representation of habitat types ranges from full sun to deep shade, rich to thin sterile soils and from dry to standing water sites. Plants are selected to provide a succession of bloom from early spring to killing frost and are sited to match the habitat that is present, rather than changing the habitat to suit the plants.

The celebration of spring begins in early April with the bright white star-like blooms of bloodroot, which arise through the folded clasp of a single leaf, and continues with the elegant uncoiling of fern fronds amongst a profusion of the sky-blue flowers of bluebells, a perennial plant native to the flood plain that will go completely dormant and disappear by midsummer.

Other spring highlights include: foamflower, wood poppy, blue phlox, smooth phlox, golden ragwort, Jacob's ladder, wild ginger, Miami mist and columbine, with native azaleas, serviceberry and fringetree as additional spring favorites.

The summer visitor will see: butterfly weed, Canada and Turk's cap lilies, dense blazing star, Culver's root, Joe-Pye weed, crimson-eyed rose mallow, and four distinctly different species of the plants commonly called black-eyed Susan.

Building up to and blooming amid the finale of fall coloration—found in tupelo, shining sumac and various viburnums and maples – are the purple New England asters, white heath asters, tickseed, sunflowers, pink turtleheads and the sun and shade-loving goldenrods.

**Brandywine Conservancy/
Brandywine River Museum
Route 1, P.O. Box 141
Chadds Ford, PA 19317
610-388-2700**

Hours: The museum is open daily, 9:30 a.m. - 4:30 p.m., and is closed Christmas Day. The gardens are open daily from 8 a.m.- 5:30 p.m. *Admission:* Fee charged for museum. Gardens admission is free.

HAGLEY MUSEUM AND LIBRARY

In 1802, E.I. du Pont chose the banks of the Brandywine on which to construct his black powder manufactory as well as a home and garden for his family. For the next 119 years, the DuPont Company's original product, black powder, was produced here.

Among industrial ruins and restorations, today's park-like museum offers more than 240 acres of history and beauty in every season. Springtime brings a vast array of blossoming trees and flowers. Autumn features the multi-colored hues of brilliant leaves viewed against towering evergreens and the meandering river.

A diversity of restorations, exhibits and live demonstrations at the museum provides a unique glimpse into nineteenth-century American life at home and at work. Demonstrations in the powder yards include a massive water wheel, a vintage steam engine and machine shop. Hagley's Blacksmith Hill is a restored worker's community that focuses on social and family history. Interpreters in period dress are cast in a foreman's home and an 1817 schoolhouse.

On a hill above what was once the world's largest black powder mills stands the charming Georgian-style 1803 residence of E.I. du Pont. It is furnished with antiques and memorabilia of the five generations of du Ponts associated with the home. Adjoining the residence is the E.I. du Pont Restored Garden – the inception of the du Pont family's rich horticultural legacy in the Brandywine Valley. The garden's French influence is reflected in the flowers, vegetables, and herbs which are grown in parterres, or sections.

Hagley Museum and Library
Route 141
Wilmington, DE 19807
302-658-2400

Hours: March 15 through December, daily 9:30 a.m. - 4:30 p.m.;
Winter hours-January through March 14, weekends, 9:30 a.m. -4:30 p.m.;
Weekdays guided tour, 1:30 p.m. Closed: Thanksgiving, Christmas and December 31.
Admission: Fee charged. Special rates for groups of fifteen or more.

LONGWOOD GARDENS

Longwood Gardens is one of the world's premier horticultural displays. Recalling the great pleasure gardens of Europe, Longwood combines horticulture, architecture, theatre, and music into a unique garden experience. Eleven thousand types of plants thrive throughout 1,050 acres of formal gardens, fountains, meadows, and woodlands. There is something happening every day, from gardening demonstrations and flower shows to Broadway musicals and lavish fireworks.

Industrialist Pierre du Pont (1870-1954) bought the property in 1906 to preserve trees planted as early as 1798 by Quaker farmers. Mr. du Pont built the major garden features enjoyed by 800,000 visitors each year.

"Welcome Spring" arrives in January, with 20 gardens blooming inside the Conservatory, including the Children's Garden, Cascade Garden, and Mediterranean Garden.

In April and May, "Acres of Spring" invites visitors outdoors to see wildflowers, gem-like bulbs, and a 600-foot-long rainbow of tulips.

Water flows dramatically in three unique fountain gardens during summer's "Festival of Fountains." Alfresco evening entertainment features music and drama in picturesque settings followed by illuminated fountain displays. On four special evenings, fireworks light up the skies.

"Autumn's Colors" peaks in October as perennial flowers bloom indoors and out and brilliant foliage flashes in Longwood's historic arboretum. Inside Mr. du Pont's former residence, the Longwood Heritage Exhibit traces the property's history.

During November's "Chrysanthemum Festival," 15,000 mums fill the Conservatory. Special performances and activities complement each year's theme.

"Christmas" blooms from Thanksgiving through New Year's Day. Thousands of brilliant poinsettias, towering evergreens, and fragrant flowers flourish in the Conservatory's warmth. In the evenings, 400,000 lights glitter outdoors and colorful fountains dance to music. Choral concerts and sing-alongs with Longwood's 10,010-pipe organ add to the holiday cheer.

Longwood is not only a beautiful site to visit, it is a wonderful place to learn. Longwood offers educational programs ranging from children's discovery stations to professional gardener training.

Longwood Gardens
Route 1, P.O. Box 501
Kennett Square, PA 19348-0501
610-388-1000

Hours: Longwood's outdoor gardens and Conservatory open at 9 a.m. and 10 a.m., respectively, every day of the year. The outdoor gardens and Conservatory close at 6 p.m. from April through October and at 5 p.m. from November through March, although both frequently are open later for special events and holiday displays.
Admission: Fee charged.

ROCKWOOD MUSEUM

Rockwood was built in 1851 by the wealthy merchant banker Joseph Shipley upon his retirement from business in England. With a rural Gothic manor designed by Liverpool architect George Williams and the Gardenesque Landscape laid out under Shipley's direction, Rockwood embodies the vision of a mid-nineteenth century English Country House. The estate was acquired by the Bringhurst branch of the family in 1892 and was maintained by the family until ownership passed to New Castle County in 1974.

Visitors to Rockwood learn about life on the estate from the turn of the century to the end of World War One. The house is especially rich in its collection of seventeenth, eighteenth and nineteenth century family furniture.

One of the unique features of the house is the attached Conservatory. This Victorian structure of cast iron and glass imported from England in the 1850s was one of the first of its type built and the last known standing. Filled with Victorian period flora in the winter months, and left empty during summer, the subtle beauty of the structure is evident. During the summer months, Conservatory plants reside on the veranda; their color and texture providing the natural segway from the stone manor to the lush park-like setting of the landscaped grounds.

The Gardenesque grounds express a simplistic natural beauty with a profusion of flowering shrubs and native and exotic trees, many of which are state champions. The ha-ha wall, pinetum and walled garden all recall the timeless beauty of an English landscape. While the beauty of the grounds at Rockwood is apparent during any season, the scents and colors of early summer are alive with blossoming roses and rhododendrons, and the spectacular colors of fall foliage are extraordinary.

Rockwood Museum
610 Shipley Road
Wilmington, DE 19809
302-761-4340

Hours: Tuesday to Sunday, 11-4 p.m., tours on the hour and half hour, the last tour offered at 3 p.m., March to December. Open Tuesday to Saturday, January and February. Closed major holidays and Mondays. Picnics are encouraged. Group rates, teas and boxed luncheons are available.
Admission: Fee charged. Prices vary during special events and exhibits. Self-guided grounds tours are free of charge. Guided grounds tours available upon request, reservations are required in advance.

UNIVERSITY OF DELAWARE
BOTANIC GARDENS

The University of Delaware Botanic Gardens (UDBG) is a collection of gardens founded in the early 1970s as a teaching resource for the Department of Plant and Soil Sciences. While containing many plants excellent for Delaware Valley landscapes, a continuing emphasis of the garden is unique plants unavailable in the trade. The new wildlife habitat garden provides visitors a natural setting in which to appreciate a mini old-field habitat. The gardens encompass ten acres surrounding the buildings of the College of Agricultural Sciences.

The UDBG mission is to promote general interest in plants and to demonstrate environmentally sound and aesthetically pleasing ways of using plants in the landscape. Education in all its facets is a top priority. The gardens are a resource for students through courses, the ornamental plant industry through special programs, and state and local residents through programs and displays.

The UDBG has plant collections for all seasons. As a test arboretum for the Holly Society of America, the UDBG has a good selection of mature hollies including recent introductions that are attractive throughout the year. Beginning in early to mid-April, the magnolias begin to flower and offer early visitors a spectacular display that continues into the summer with the large-leafed native species. Viburnums brighten the spring garden with their attractive and sometimes fragrant flowers. The herbaceous garden provides summer color and many examples of annual and perennial plants for the home garden. Plant interest continues into the autumn with the colorful fruit of shrubs and vibrant fall foliage of trees.

University of Delaware Botanic Gardens
Department of Plant and Soil Sciences
University of Delaware
Newark, DE 19717
302-831-2531

Hours: The University of Delaware Botanic Gardens are open to the public daily from sunrise to sunset.
Admission: No charge for admission. A visitor's information kiosk is located at the south end of Townsend Hall. The UDBG offers a variety of self-guided tours, brochures, and special horticultural collections for the visitor.

WINTERTHUR MUSEUM, GARDEN AND LIBRARY

For many, the name Winterthur evokes images of a world-class museum of American decorative arts. But one of Winterthur's greatest treasures lies just beyond the museum walls – a glorious, naturalistic garden.

The former country estate of Henry Francis du Pont (1880-1969), Winterthur opened to the public in 1951. Decades before du Pont bought his first antique, he studied horticulture, agriculture, botany and landscape design. Working with landscape architect Marian Cruger Coffin and the garden staff, he created a masterpiece inspired by the natural landscape of the Brandywine Valley.

Today, a walk through the garden is a delight at any time of year, from the floral beauty of spring to the brilliant colors of autumn. The first spring flowers appear on the March Bank as early as February. The area features thousands of bulbs, including spring snowflakes, winter aconite and glory-of-the-snow. The family's tennis and croquet courts became the semi-formal Sundial Garden, at its most eye-catching and fragrant in April. Highlights of this area include Chinese snowball viburnums, flowering quinces and lilacs. Azaleas are among the most widely used plants at Winterthur. They appear throughout the garden, but are the stars of the eight-acre Azalea Woods, at its peak of beauty around Mother's Day. Banks of red, white and pink azaleas create a lush cathedral of blossoms during the month of May.

The Peony Garden has magnificent flowers in shades that range from golden yellow, ethereal white and palest lavender to dark rose, brilliant scarlet and deep blackish maroon. The Quarry Garden features thirteen species of primula blooming through late May and early June, accented by the blue and yellow blossoms of irises. Hostas and lobelias bloom in July and August, while the fall palette features pink anemones, pink turtle-head and yellow ligularia.

Winterthur Museum, Garden, and Library
Route 52
Winterthur, DE 19735
800-448-3883
302-888-4600

Hours: The garden is open 9 a.m. to dusk, Monday to Saturday; noon to dusk, Sunday. Winterthur is closed Christmas, New Year's and Thanksgiving Days.
Admission: Fee charged. All admission tickets include a garden tram ride and self-guided tour of the garden. Some museum tours require reservations.

27. Bowman's Hill Wildflower Preserve
28. Historic Fallsington, Inc.
29. Medford Leas, The Lewis W. Barton
    Arboretum and Nature Preserve
30. The Henry Schmieder Arboretum of
    Delaware Valley College

Bucks County is full of stunning farms, charming villages and wonderful open spaces. Known for its historic houses, antique shops and artist studios, visitors can follow the meandering Delaware Canal through one of the most exquisite areas of the Northeast. Bowman's Hill Wildflower Preserve offers an outstanding naturalistic setting. Historic Fallsington presents a unique community where people have lived and worked for more than 300 years. The Henry Schmieder Arboretum of Delaware Valley College is set in a farmland setting near the county seat of Doylestown. Medford Leas, the Lewis W. Barton Arboretum and Nature Preserve, provides a variety of naturalistic gardens and courtyards integrated into the life of residents.

BOWMAN'S HILL WILDFLOWER PRESERVE

In 1934, Pennsylvania established its first wildflower preserve at Bowman's Hill. Since its inception, Bowman's Hill Wildflower Preserve has dedicated itself to educating the public about the importance of preserving native plants. As a subdivision of the 500-acre complex of Washington Crossing Historic Park and an accredited member of the American Association of Museums, the Preserve is a living memorial to the patriots of George Washington's army who camped in the area during the American Revolutionary War.

The 100 acres of rolling hillside crossed by Pidcock Creek provide diverse and picturesque habitats. The meadows and forests, springs and dry uplands, as well as man-made habitats supply the conditions necessary to grow more than 800 species of native wildflowers, ferns, trees, shrubs and vines. Of special interest are the more than eighty species listed as plants of special concern in Pennsylvania and the United States.

Each season features special attractions. Winter closes with the emerging spathes of skunk cabbage challenging snow cover. Soon to follow are blooms of trillium, spring beauty, and trout lilies. Virginia bluebells color the flood plains in April and May. Before the summer canopy is complete, spring shrubs blossom. The native azaleas burst into color and fragrance. Meadow flowers bask in the summer sun, pursued by eager pollinators and butterflies. Visitors and shade-loving flowers find respite from the heat along wooded paths. Acres of trees and shrubs become a medley of fall color. Leaf-fall exposes the quiet silhouettes of woody plants for winter study.

The Preserve provides excellent outdoor opportunities to study nesting and migrating birds. The Sinkler Observation Area allows indoor bird study and the Platt Collection allows year-round study of taxidermied birds, nests and eggs. The Headquarters Building is the hub for diverse botanical displays and programs.

The Park is administered by the Pennsylvania Historic and Museum Commission and the Washington Crossing Park Commission with Bowman's Hill Wildflower Preserve Association.

Bowman's Hill Wildflower Preserve
Washington Crossing Historic Park
P.O. Box 685
New Hope, PA 18938-0685
215-862-2924

Hours: The building is open Tuesday through Saturday from 9 a.m.- 5 p.m. Sundays the building is open from noon-5 p.m. Closed Mondays (except Monday holidays), Easter, Christmas Day, New Year's Day, Thanksgiving and the day after. Trails open until dusk.
Admission: No charge for admission.

HISTORIC FALLSINGTON, INC.

Historic Fallsington, Inc. is a private nonprofit historic preservation organization and museum that has been conserving and sharing the 300-year-old village of Fallsington since 1953. The village, which consists of over ninety historic buildings from the eighteenth and nineteenth centuries, was significant as a religious, social and market center for the surrounding community, as well as a stopover for stagecoach travelers. William Penn, while in residence at nearby Pennsbury Manor, attended religious services in Fallsington.

Historic Fallsington, Inc. has preserved six historic buildings. The Moon-Williamson Log House is a hand-hewn structure which served as the home of Samuel Moon, a well-known carpenter and joiner in the late decades of the eighteenth century. Boasting one of the most beautiful doorways in Bucks County, the Burges-Lippincott House is a Federal period house and was the home of the Village doctor, Dr. Henry Lippincott, in the nineteenth century. The Stagecoach Tavern operated as a tavern from 1799 until Prohibition forced its doors to close. The Schoolmaster's House was constructed in 1758 for the schoolmaster employed by the Falls Monthly Meeting of Friends. Circa 1910, the Gillingham General Store houses the headquarters and museum store of Historic Fallsington, Inc. and the Gambrel Roof House is a 1728 Friends Meetinghouse still standing on the old town square.

The village of Fallsington is a beautiful destination all year long. Herb, flower and vegetable gardens thrive in the spring and summer and in autumn Fallsington's old trees come alive with fall color. Private homes as well as Fallsington's museum buildings take pride in their plantings. Heritage roses are a part of the historic landscape of the tavern. The tavern grounds are also the location of an ongoing herb project which includes an informational brochure and cooking programs. Visitors exploring the byways of the village come to feel the sense of a gentler time.

The village of Fallsington is on the National Register of Historic Places and is the only village in Bucks County which is organized to actively interpret and preserve its history.

Historic Fallsington, Inc.
4 Yardley Avenue
Fallsington, PA 19054
215-295-6567

Hours: May through October hours are Monday-Saturday, 10 a.m. -4 p.m. and Sunday, noon-4 p.m. for guided tours. Museum Store and offices are open Monday-Saturday, 9 a.m. - 5 p.m. and Sunday, noon-5 p.m. until December 24. January, February and March hours are Monday-Friday, 9 a.m. - 5 p.m.
Admission: Fee charged. Group rates available upon request.

MEDFORD LEAS, THE LEWIS W. BARTON ARBORETUM AND NATURE PRESERVE

Medford Leas, created in 1981, contains 160 acres of landscaped grounds, courtyard gardens, wildflower meadows, natural woodlands and wetlands. Within the Arboretum are collections of trees and shrubs from many parts of the world. The Nature Preserve includes mature upland oak, birch, and hickory woods typical of the forest cover once dominant on the Inner Coastal Plain in New Jersey. Along the southwest branch of the Rancocas Creek, which borders one section of the Preserve, is a flood plain forest in which red maple, sweet gum, tulip and ironwood trees are prominent. The largest hickory tree in New Jersey is also located in this area.

One outstanding collection is the Pinetum, a group of cone-bearing trees, mostly evergreen, including such exotic trees as the Bosnian pine, the Himalayan pine, the Nordman fir, and the Japanese umbrella tree. The extensive collection of hollies includes some dwarf varieties and a lovely holly that is over forty-feet tall. There are thirty-four "Courtyard Gardens" that have been individually designed by a number of talented landscape architects and horticulturists. Each "Courtyard Garden" is handicapped accessible and benches are conveniently located along the walkways and trails. There is adjacent signage that identifies the plant materials. The large rhododendron garden is shaded by a canopy of tall trees and under-planted with native wildflowers and ferns. Over sixty-eight acres of meadow are abloom with wildflowers and thousands of daffodils edge the roads and walking paths.

Spring and early summer are particularly beautiful with flowering bulbs, shrubs, trees and wildflowers. In addition, many trees and shrubs have been selected because of their rich fall leaf color or vibrant berries.

Medford Leas, The Lewis W. Barton Arboretum and Nature Preserve
Route 70 (1/4 mile east of Rt. 541)
Medford, NJ 08055
609-654-3000

Hours: The Arboretum is open 365 days a year from 9 a.m. until dusk.
Admission: No charge for admission. Register at the reception desk where there are tour maps.

THE HENRY SCHMIEDER ARBORETUM OF DELAWARE VALLEY COLLEGE

The vision for the Henry Schmieder Arboretum dates back to the founding of Delaware Valley College as The National Farm School in 1896 by Philadelphia Rabbi Joseph Krauskopf. It was not until 1966 however, that the Arboretum was formally given a name, the Henry Schmieder Arboretum, in honor of one of the College's most revered professors.

The Arboretum encompasses the entire main campus area. Plant collections have been deftly incorporated into the campus landscape giving visitors an opportunity to see and study plants in a landscape setting. Historic buildings and century-old trees provide a unique framework for the Arboretum's collections. The Arboretum serves as an outdoor laboratory for teaching and research. Special "eduscapes" and collection gardens have been designed to help students and visitors study annuals, ornamental grasses, herbs, vines, rare conifers, daylilies, native plants, shade plants and plants with winter interest.

While there is always something to see and learn at the Henry Schmieder Arboretum, spring and summer are the most colorful times to visit. An impressive display of thousands of spring flowering bulbs is followed by the beauty of over one hundred different cultivars of daylily. The show and education continues with the color of an extensive display of annuals. The recently completed Gazebo Garden provides an ideal spot to study annuals and annual vines. The Arboretum's new, completely rebuilt Lois Burpee Herb Garden shines throughout the growing season with a vast collection of culinary, medicinal, fragrance, dye, industrial and other useful plants. A self-guided tour will take you to these areas as well as The Woodland Walk, The Winter Walk, The Hilman Family Garden, various campus landscapes and collections as well as The 1920s Cottage Garden, The Jean Work Garden and Centennial Landscape which showcase ecologically sound design and the integration of native plants into the landscape.

The Henry Schmieder Arboretum
of Delaware Valley College
700 East Butler Avenue (Route 202)
Doylestown, PA 18901-2697
215-489-2283

Hours: Dawn to dusk every day-except holidays. Greenhouses open week-days only.
Admission: No charge for admission. Self-guided tour available. Fee for guided tours-guided tours by appointment only. Call for lecture/workshop series information.

Philadelphia and Northwest Suburbs (PA)

1. Awbury Arboretum
2. Cliveden of the National Trust
3. The Highlands Mansion & Gardens
4. Historic Bartram's Garden
5. Japanese House and Garden (Shōfusō, The Pine Breeze Villa)
6. Ebenezer Maxwell Mansion Victorian Gardens
7. Morris Arboretum of the University of Pennsylvania
8. The Woodlands
9. Wyck

Main Line (PA)

10. The American College Arboretum
11. The Barnes Foundation Arboretum
12. Chanticleer
13. Haverford College Arboretum
14. The Henry Foundation for Botanical Research
15. Jenkins Arboretum
16. Arboretum Villanova

Delaware County (PA)

17. The Grange Estate
18. Scott Arboretum of Swarthmore College
19. Taylor Memorial Arboretum
20. Tyler Arboretum

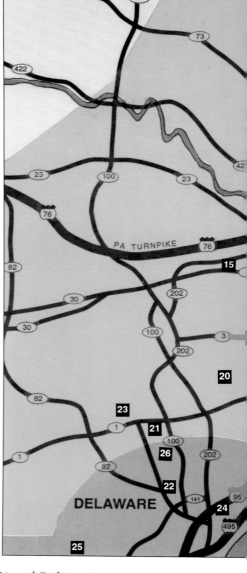

Brandywine Area: Chester County (PA) and Delaware

✓21. Brandywine Conservancy / Brandywine River Museum
✓22. Hagley Museum and Library
✓23. Longwood Gardens
24. Rockwood Museum
25. University of Delaware Botanic Gardens
✓26. Winterthur Museum, Garden, and Library